DATE DUE

FEB 2 2 2018			

Demco, Inc. 38-293

Why it works

Light and Dark

Anna Claybourne

QEB Publishing

How far can you see?

Guess how far your eyes can see. One mile? Ten miles? One hundred thousand miles?

It's further than that! At night, you can see the Moon. It is about 248,550 miles away from the Earth.

From the top of a hill or a tall building you can see a very long way, if nothing blocks your view.

At night, you can see the stars. They are millions of miles away. Like the Sun, each star is a ball of fire. You can see the stars because light from them travels to your eyes.

Light moves very fast. It travels about 186,400 miles every second!

Light moves much faster than speedy space rockets.

Shadows

Shine a flashlight at a wall, then put your hands in the way. What happens?

Your hands block the light from the flashlight and make a shadow on the wall.

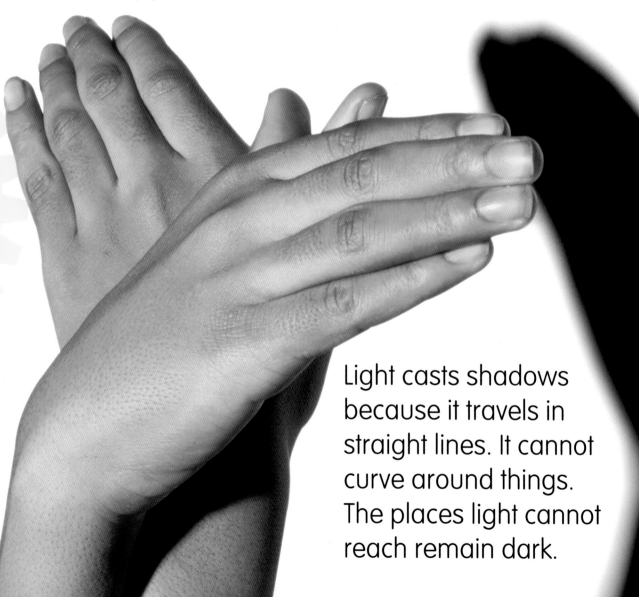

Light casts shadows because it travels in straight lines. It cannot curve around things. The places light cannot reach remain dark.

A shadow forms when an object stops light getting through.

Beam of light

Flashlight

Shadow

It's a fact

As the rays of light shine out of the flashlight they spread out in straight lines. This makes the spider's shadow on the wall bigger than the spider itself.

Bouncing light

Light travels in straight lines. To go round a corner, it must bounce off something.

Light bounces off things all the time. For example, it can bounce, or reflect, off a mirror.

Try this

Try this experiment to see round a corner. You need a small plastic mirror.

1 Stand outside a room, next to the doorway, so that you cannot see inside.

2 Hold up the mirror so that it faces the room. Turn it slowly toward you. You will be able to see things inside the room reflected in the mirror.

It's a fact

Light from the Sun or another source bounces off objects in the room, then hits the mirror. The light bounces off the mirror into your eyes. This lets you see everything around you including around corners!

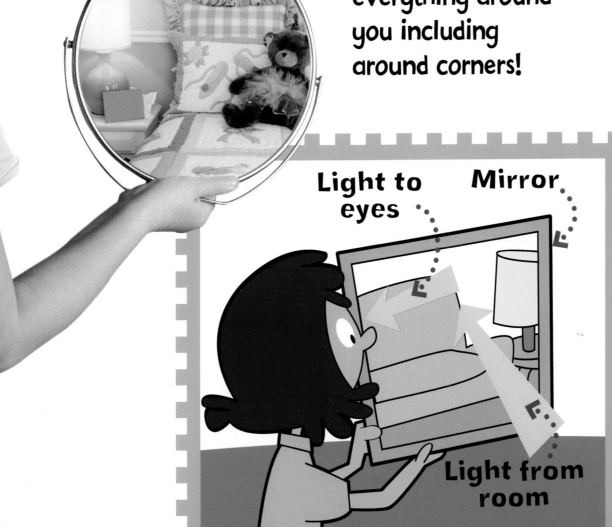

Light to eyes

Mirror

Light from room

Bending light

Light can bend when it passes in and out of see-through substances, such as water and plastic. This is called refraction.

Try this

The way light bends can make a coin seem to move! You need a coin, a clear bowl, some water, and an adult to help you.

1 Put the coin in the bottom of the bowl. Sit facing the bowl so that you can see it from one side.

It's a fact

You see the coin because light bouncing off it travels to your eyes in a straight line.

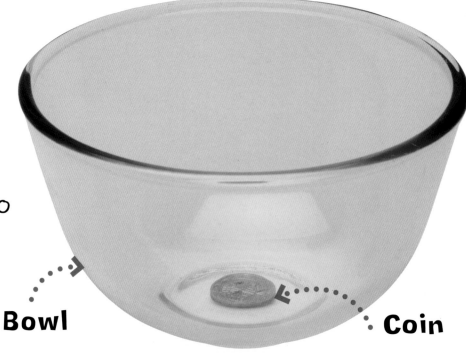

Bowl

Coin

Water often looks shallower when you stand in a swimming pool. Your legs look shorter, too. This happens because of refraction.

If you stand a pencil in a glass of water, refraction makes it look broken.

2 Keep very still and ask the adult to slowly fill the bowl with water. The coin seems to rise up, although it is still on the bottom.

With water in the bowl, the light bends as it passes from water to air. It makes the coin look as though it has moved.

Water

15

Night on Earth

Why does it get dark at night? Our planet, the Earth, is spinning. As it spins, the area that we live in slowly faces toward the Sun, then turns away again.

Try this

You can see how this works using a flashlight, a ball, and a sticker.

1 Place the sticker on the ball to stand for the area where you live.

2 Make the room dark and shine the flashlight at the ball. Now spin the ball around.

3 As the ball spins, the sticker moves into the light, then the dark. The Earth does the same.

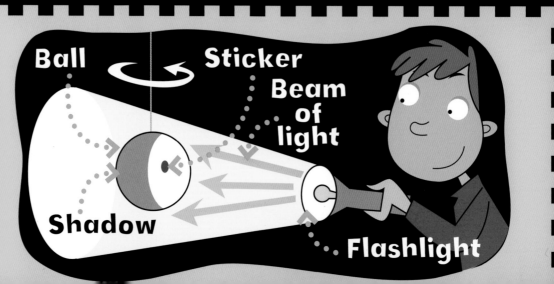

Ball Sticker Beam of light

Shadow

Flashlight

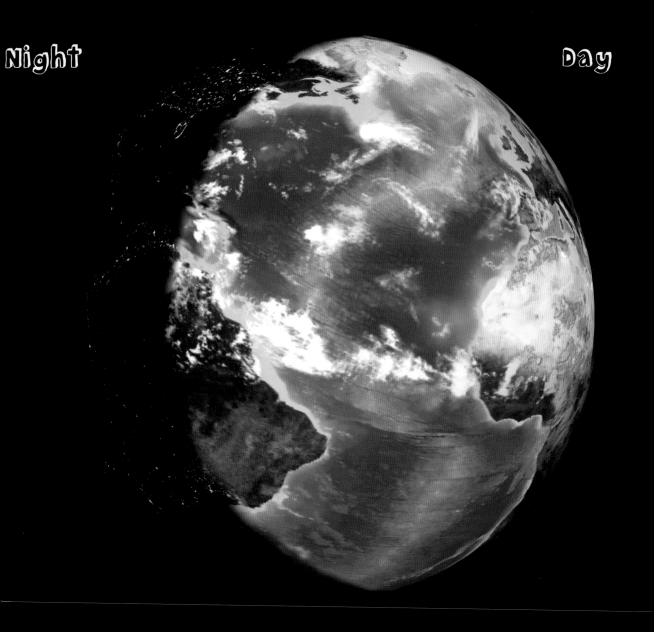

When we're in the light, it's daytime. When we face away from the Sun, it's night.

It's a fact

Light cannot curve around the Earth. So the part facing away from the Sun is in shadow. The Sun does not switch off. It is always daytime somewhere in the world.

17

Shadow clock

Throughout the day, the Sun seems to move across the sky. This makes shadows move, too.

Try this

Make a shadow clock to tell the time. You will need a pencil, a straw, modeling clay, a paper plate, and a clock or watch.

1 Use modeling clay to stick the straw onto the middle of the plate, standing straight up.

Paper plate

Modeling clay

Straw

Watch

Pencil

2 Put the plate in a sunny place, such as a windowsill where the sun shines for most of the day.

3 Every hour, mark where the straw's shadow falls and label it with the time.

Paper plate

Straw

Modeling clay

3pm

2pm

1pm

12pm

4 Keep the clock in the same position. Now you can use your clock to tell the time.

For example, whenever the shadow falls on the mark for 3 o'clock, it is 3 o'clock!

A sundial is a kind of shadow clock, usually made of stone and metal. People used sundials to tell the time before there were ticking clocks.

The colors of light

Light from lamps and from the Sun looks white. It is actually made of many colors mixed together.

Try this

You can see the colors of light if you shine light through a triangle-shaped piece of glass or plastic, called a prism.

You will need: a flashlight, a piece of white paper, and a prism.

1 Shine the flashlight through the prism.

2 Hold the paper on the other side of the prism. Can you see all the colors?

A rainbow forms when raindrops act like tiny prisms. They split up white sunlight into all its colors.

It's a fact

As the light passes into and out of the prism, it bends, or refracts. This makes the light split into many colors.

Glossary

Daylight
Light from the Sun that shines on us during the day.

Electricity
A kind of energy that can be used to make machines work.

Energy
The power to make things work, happen, or move.

Light source
Something that gives out light, such as a flashlight or lamp.

Prism
A triangular piece of glass or clear plastic. When light shines into and out of a prism, it bends and splits into separate colors.

Pupil
The black hole in your eye that lets in light.

Reflect
To bounce off a surface and change direction. Light reflects off mirrors and other objects.

Refraction
The way light bends when it passes from one see-through substance into another.

Shadow
An area of darkness that is made when an object blocks the path of light.

Index

Notes for parents and teachers

• For all activities involving sunlight, remind children never to look directly at the Sun, as it can damage eyesight.

• Look out for shadows in everyday situations. Discuss the conditions that create sharp shadows, such as bright sunlight or a strong, single light source. If there are a lot of lights in a room, or if the Sun is behind clouds and its light is spread out across the sky, shadows become blurred or unclear. Discuss with children why this might be.

• See how many light sources children can see at any one time, including the Sun, electric lights, candlelight, and small LED lights on phones, watches, and computers. They could make a list of all the light sources they can find and describe whether the light is white or colored, and whether they think it is bright or dim.

• Planets and the Moon seem to shine in the night sky, but they are not light sources. Encourage children to work out why this may be. Planets and the Moon reflect light from the Sun, making it bounce back to us on Earth. This happens even when we can't see the Sun. So moonlight is actually light from the Sun, reflecting back at us.

• Encourage children to look in a mirror. Ask "Why can you see yourself?" Light bounces from a light source off you, and hits the mirror. It reflects back off the mirror and into your eyes.

• For another refraction experiment, dip a straw into a glass of water. Bend it this way and that, and look at it from different angles. It will sometimes appear bent because refraction bends the light traveling from it.